spot

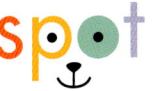

BABY FARM ANIMALS

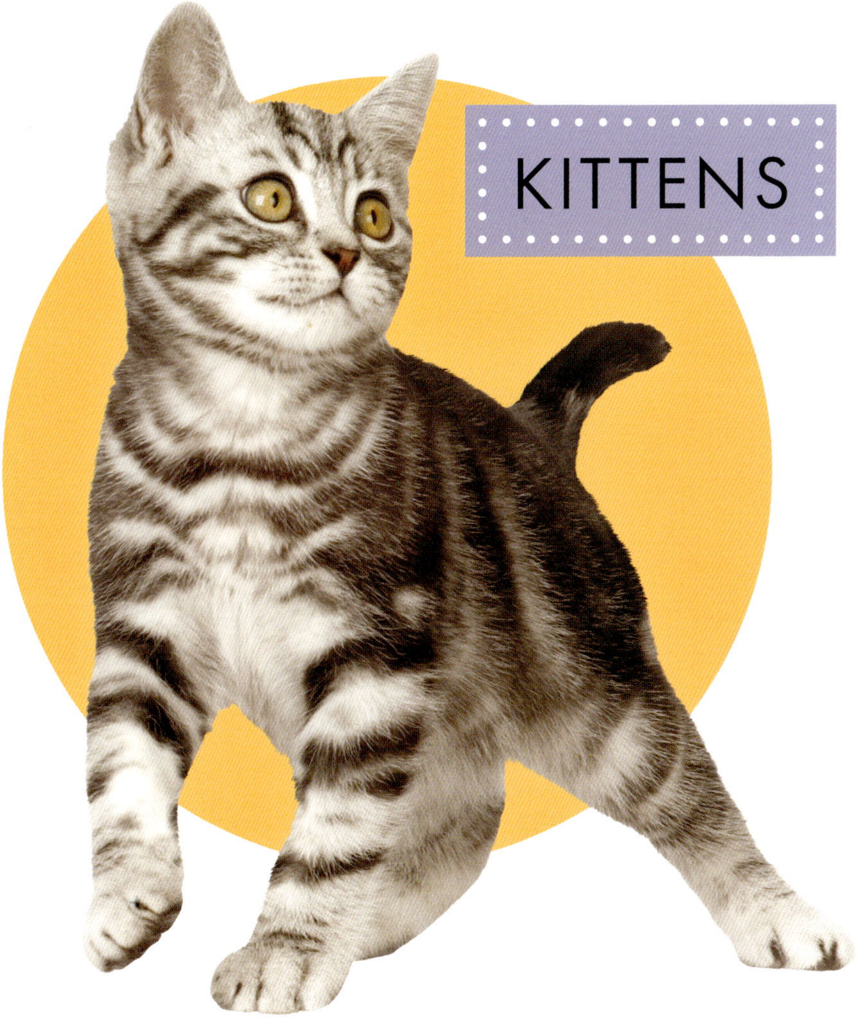

KITTENS

by Anastasia Suen

AMICUS | AMICUS INK

eyes  tail

Look for these words and pictures as you read.

teeth paw

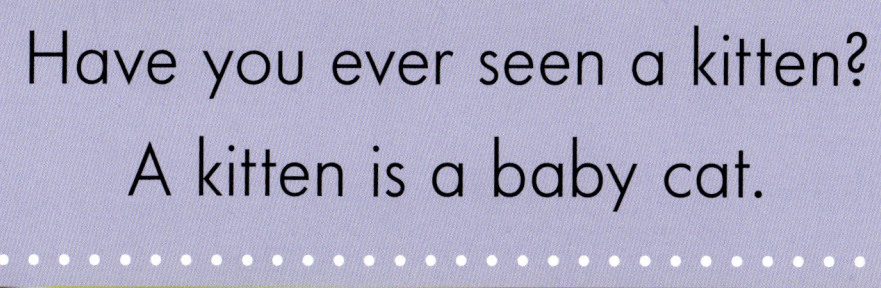

Have you ever seen a kitten?
A kitten is a baby cat.

Many kittens are born at once. The group is called a litter.

Look at the kitten's eyes.
They will not open for a week.

eyes

Look at the kitten's tail.
It is long.
It helps the kitten balance.

tail

Look at the kitten's teeth.
They are sharp.
They help the kitten hunt.

teeth

Look at the kitten's paw.
It has toes.
It has claws.

paw

A kitten will grow up.
It will live with other cats.
The farm cats hunt mice.

eyes

tail

Did you find?

teeth

paw

Spot is published by Amicus and Amicus Ink
P.O. Box 1329, Mankato, MN 56002
www.amicuspublishing.us

Copyright © 2019 Amicus.
International copyright reserved in all countries.
No part of this book may be reproduced in any form without written permission from the publisher.

Names: Suen, Anastasia, author.
Title: Kittens / by Anastasia Suen.
Description: Mankato, MN : Amicus/Amicus Ink, [2019] | Series: Spot. Baby farm animals | "Spot is published by Amicus." | Audience: K to grade 3.
Identifiers: LCCN 2017053725 (print) | LCCN 2017054237 (ebook) | ISBN 9781681515717 (pdf) | ISBN 9781681515335 (library binding) | ISBN 9781681523712 (pbk.)
Subjects: LCSH: Kittens--Juvenile literature. | Farms--Juvenile literature. | Vocabulary.
Classification: LCC SF445.7 (ebook) | LCC SF445.7 .S84 2019 (print) | DDC 636.8/07--dc23
LC record available at https://lccn.loc.gov/2017053725

Printed in China

HC 10 9 8 7 6 5 4 3 2 1
PB 10 9 8 7 6 5 4 3 2 1

Wendy Dieker and
 Mary Ellen Klukow, editors
Deb Miner, series designer
Aubrey Harper, book designer
Holly Young, photo researcher

Photos by iStock/GlobalP, cover, 1, 16, anurakpong, 2, 6–7, 15, v777999, 2, 10–11, 15, s_derevianko, 2, 12–13, 15, annaia, 3; Alamy/Juniors Bildarchiv/F240, 2, 8–9, 15, syliva born, 14; iStock/Nata-K, 4–5